THE DEPARTMENT OF HOMELAND SECURITY

FIGHTING TERRORISM

David Baker

Rourke
Publishing LLC
Vero Beach, Florida 32964

www.rourkepublishing.com

PHOTO CREDITS: p. 18: Adam DuBrowa/FEMA News Photo; p. 31: FBI; p. 16: Nicholas Kamm/AFP/Getty Images; p. 10 National Park Service, U.S. Department of the Interior; pp. 11, 15: Photodisc/Getty Images; p. 7: Bill Pugliano/Getty Images; pp. 6 (Staff Sgt. Gary Coppage), 17 (Capt. Jim Fabio), 41 (George Rolhmaller): U.S. Air Force; pp. 40 (PA3 Sabrina Arrayan), 4 (PAC Brandon Brewer), 27, 28, 35 (PO Mike Lutz), 39: U.S. Coast Guard; pp. 12, 21, 23, 24, 38, 42 (Gerald L. Nino), 13, 14 (both), 30 (both), 43 (James Tourtellotte), 26 (K. L. Wong): U.S. Customs and Border Protection; pp. 20 (Photographer's Mate 2nd Class Richard J. Brunson), 33 (Photographer's Mate 2nd Class Jason P. Taylor): U.S. Navy; p. 9: Mark Wilson/ Getty Images

Title page picture shows the ruins of the Twin Towers in New York City after the terrorist attacks of September 11, 2001.

Produced for Rourke Publishing by Discovery Books
Editor: Paul Humphrey
Designer: Ian Winton
Photo researcher: Rachel Tisdale

Library of Congress Cataloging-in-Publication Data

Baker, David, 1944-
  The Department of Homeland Security / by David Baker.
    p. cm. -- (Fighting terrorism)
  Includes index.
  ISBN 1-59515-484-1
  1. United States. Dept. of Homeland Security--Juvenile literature. 2. Terrorism--United States--Prevention--Juvenile literature. 3. National security--United States--Juvenile literature. I. Title.
  HV6432.B335 2006
  363.320973--dc22
                                        2005028175

Printed in the USA

TABLE OF CONTENTS

Chapter One

A Challenge to Freedom

On September 11, 2001, the United States was hit by terrorists who hijacked four commercial airliners. They crashed two of them into the World Trade Center in New York City, one into the Pentagon, near Washington, D.C., and a fourth into the ground in Pennsylvania when passengers attempted to take control of the hijacked aircraft. This was a day in which nearly 3,000 people died at the hands of suicide **fanatics**, a dreadful day that changed the way we all view security and the right to protection from our government.

FACT FILE ★

The events of 9/11 showed that there are many groups around the world, and some countries, that are determined to extinguish those democratic aspirations and to prevent individuals standing up for human rights.

In times of war the Department of Defense protects the interests of the United States, the lives of its people, and the right to move freely in our own country without the threat of invasion. Yet, in a single day, the terrible events that took the lives of ordinary people changed how we think of threats to our way of life and to our freedoms.

Of course, Americans have been attacked in many places around the world for many years. There have always been terrorist groups determined to seize by force what they are unable to get through negotiation and debate. In the United

(Opposite) The still-smoldering World Trade Center complex in New York City on September 26, 2001, just two weeks after the terrorist attacks that stunned the world.

Helicopters and ambulances help ferry the wounded to the hospital following the terrorist attack on the Pentagon, September 11, 2001.

States we believe in the rights of people everywhere to live in freedom and to enjoy the benefits of democracy.

We believe that all citizens count and should have a voice in the sort of government they want and who, from among them, they want to represent them. Americans have always tried to send that message to other countries where oppression and torture prevent freedom and democracy. This is why Americans often come under attack and why citizens of our allies are also frequently in danger from fanatics unable to understand these values and who are incapable of behaving in a responsible and democratic way.

The right to vote a government in or out is the fundamental principle of a democracy, and one that many terrorist organizations seek to destroy.

Chapter Two

Securing the Nation

The immediate response of the government to September 11 was to secure the land, sea, and air routes into and out of the United States. Almost immediately all aircraft were grounded, and all movements on land and water were restrained. The Department of Defense went on alert—just in case the four airliner hijackings were the beginning of a larger attack.

At first it was unclear where the attack had come from. A great shock was the realization that the attack had, in fact, come from within the United States itself. While Americans took cautionary steps to look after their security in foreign countries, helped by embassies and offices of the State Department, it was disturbing to realize that terrorists could infiltrate our borders and prepare to attack us from within.

Our government responded to these realities quickly and with the awareness that something very different was needed to secure the United States from further attacks. The Homeland and Security Act of 2002 was just such a response and served to mobilize the nation and the people in a focused effort.

President George W. Bush and members of Congress in the White House following the signing into law of the November 25, 2002 Homeland and Security Act.

In Congress there was debate about how best to meet the new threats. Some wanted stiffer border controls, virtually closing down the country to seal it from **infiltrators**. Others sought strong **reprisal** attacks against those countries known to harbor terrorists and wanted a military response to the events of 9/11.

Yet America is an open society where people go about their daily business. It is against the principles of American democracy to deny people the right to enter our country unless they plan

The United States has usually welcomed immigrants to our shores. However, the recent terrorist outrages have strengthened the need for tighter border controls.

harm or criminal activities. In a way, said many around the country in federal and local government, to seal the United States would be to send a signal to the terrorists that they had won.

So it was agreed to set up a Department of Homeland Security (DHS)—one unifying body to link all the many government institutions essential to the protection of not only the country and its people but also the people we welcome to our nation as visitors.

Out of the Homeland and Security Act of 2002 came the Department of Homeland Security, which formally came into being on March 1, 2003. It became the 15th department in the federal government and gathered together 22 agencies merged into a single unit that collectively employs 180,000 people. The vision set forth by the Act was to preserve the freedoms of the United States, to protect the nation, and to make the homeland safe. Its mission was to lead a unified effort from existing government agencies, to secure the borders, to welcome lawful immigrants and visitors, and to ensure the free flow of commerce.

For a country like America it is important that trade flows freely. We build our wealth on the exchange of goods and the flow of commercial transactions. It is important that business

New York Harbor before the terrorist attacks of September 11, 2001, showing the Twin Towers of the World Trade Center in the background. Keeping terrorists out and trade flowing is a difficult challenge for the DHS.

people as well as tourists and visitors are allowed to move around freely. It is also important that we have a defense against those who come as though they are friends but in fact carry murderous intentions.

The core values of the Department of Homeland Security are based around personal attributes encouraged in every citizen and are qualities every one of us should aspire to possess.

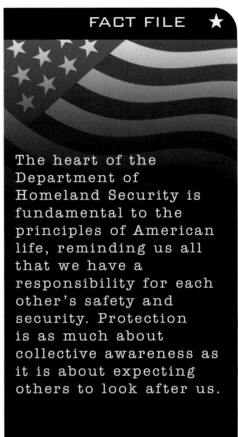

The heart of the Department of Homeland Security is fundamental to the principles of American life, reminding us all that we have a responsibility for each other's safety and security. Protection is as much about collective awareness as it is about expecting others to look after us.

Secretary Tom Ridge announces the new Homeland Security seal to DHS employees in Selfridge, Michigan, June 2003.

Secretary Ridge at the launch of US-VISIT, Atlanta, Georgia, May 2004.

These are *integrity*, *vigilance*, and *respect*. Instilling *integrity*, the Department reminds us all that each of its members serves something greater than ourselves, including the president and his administration.

With the motto "service before self" it sets high standards for itself and pledges to act in the knowledge that, at the point of entry to the United States, the first Americans a visitor sees are representatives of the Department. The Department pledges itself to *vigilance* by identifying and deterring threats to the United States and its people. Finally, *respect* for the Department means building valuable relationships with customers, partners, and stakeholders to honor founding concepts of America such as liberty, democracy, and civil rights.

During its first year the DHS introduced a new program aimed at screening illegal immigrants and even caught known criminals trying to get back into the country. This program is called US-VISIT, and stands for United States Visitor and

In January 2004 the DHS introduced biometric data recording machines at all points of entry into the United States.

Immigrant Status Indicator Technology. This was first introduced at large airports and incorporated **biometric** data recording machines.

These machines take information and biomedical data unique to that individual and are often the only possible way to identify an individual who is seeking to conceal his or her true identity. This technology is very important when dealing with people skilled in avoiding detection. **Counterfeit** identities can be provided by skilled forgers who create false documents and give people new backgrounds that only biometric information can detect. In the year beginning in January 2004 the biometric capability of US-VISIT apprehended 107 people wanted for previous crimes.

Other areas enhanced during the first year of operation for the DHS included port security, whereby 17 key distribution centers got special security grants to beef up their controls with something called threat mapping. This is a technical capability to gather a lot of information and analyze it so that specialized teams can be deployed to potential targets to stiffen defensive measures or build up protective forces.

Potential targets could be anything from the waterfront in Boston, Massachusetts, to the White House in Washington, D.C. Understanding where threats may appear is an important step toward preventing another disaster. All of these operational units are controlled from a central Homeland Security Operations Center, where 26 federal and law enforcement agencies work together with intelligence community members who operate 24 hours a day, 7 days a week.

The Boston waterfront. Our coastal cities are particularly at risk from seaborne attack by terrorists.

Chapter Three

The Role of the Citizen

In a program known as the Ready Campaign and Citizen Corps, the DHS encouraged ordinary people to contribute to homeland security by improving their awareness of their environment, to be vigilant, and to train for emergency support. When terrorists strike they can cause damage and loss of life, and emergency services can be swamped by demands for medical assistance and firefighters.

Volunteers in Washington's Metro Citizen Corps Volunteer Emergency Response Program and their police escorts at a training session inside a Metro tunnel, May 11, 2005.

It is helpful to have citizens informed about the best way to help the emergency services and to come to the assistance of each other, to know basic medical aid, and to understand how to get the right help they need. An emergency can happen at any time, and local communities have been stimulated to get involved in emergency

Firefighters at the World Trade Center, September 11, 2001. When the emergency services become overstretched during a terrorist attack, they can count on help from the Citizen Corps.

preparedness. In the first year after the DHS set up the program in 2003, more than 900 communities formed emergency preparedness councils.

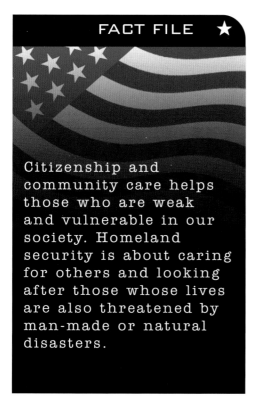

FACT FILE ★

Citizenship and community care helps those who are weak and vulnerable in our society. Homeland security is about caring for others and looking after those whose lives are also threatened by man-made or natural disasters.

Getting citizens involved in national defense against terror and equipping them to assist themselves and others in times of emergency was stimulated by the addition of $8 billion to support state and local preparedness efforts. Also, the newly formed Homeland Security Center of Excellence and Fellows fostered development of new technologies and research for the first such facility set up at the University of Southern California. Here, the inaugural class of 100 students was dedicated to researching and developing new technologies for citizen protection and the general security of the homeland.

In a program called State and Local Preparedness Coordination, all levels of government were brought closer together to cooperate and combine resources in times of emergency. This had beneficial results when hurricanes struck, and wildfires in California—together with the worst tornado season in years—brought an unexpected use to the program during 2003.

Federal Emergency Management Agency (FEMA) officials examine a building in Gladstone, Missouri, following the May 2003 tornadoes.

Chapter Four

Consolidating Security

During the second year of its activity, the DHS drew up a specific set of priorities based on performance and activity during its first 12 months. For the period beginning March 2004 it was to provide stronger information sharing and expand its database. This involved expanding the computer-based information network to all 50 states, five territories, Washington, D.C., and 50 other major urban areas.

To increase and protect critical **infrastructure**, the DHS had set up by December 2004 a national database of resources, tools, and critical equipment essential to combat threats. In the event of an emergency, it is vital that not only the right people but also the correct equipment are distributed to the appropriate locations. Such a database is vital for making sure that happens.

New programs to bring military-style operations to homeland security were introduced with tests using unmanned aerial vehicles (UAVs). These are unmanned flying machines that look like model airplanes and are controlled by an operator located at a central facility. UAVs can be flown remotely in countries other than the United States and controlled by an operator

The Lockheed P-3 has been of service to the U.S. military for over 45 years. Today it is used for long-range surveillance work.

several thousand miles away. UAVs can carry special equipment to take images in day or night conditions and patrol remote regions or borders.

Using unmanned equipment like this, security officers can keep watch on places where terrorists might sneak in undetected. Conventional piloted aircraft such as the specially equipped long-range Lockheed P-3 surveillance aircraft are now being used to support counter-drug and counter-terrorism efforts. The Lockheed P-3 has been around a long time. It was flown for the first time in 1959 and has served the U.S. Navy with distinction as an anti-submarine aircraft. It has great range and can remain in the air for a long time.

Technology such as unmanned aerial vehicles has been in development for a long time and unmanned aircraft like these have been used by the Department of Defense to project a military presence in dangerous areas where human life would be at great risk. UAVs are also used to patrol remote areas

This unmanned aerial vehicle (UAV) stands ready for action on the U.S. southern border.

where access by road is difficult or impossible. They have been used extensively in places such as Afghanistan and in remote areas of Iraq. In the case of their use by the DHS, government officers are able to save money and increase the speed with which data can be obtained and returned to the central control facility.

UAVs can carry a wide range of technical equipment including cameras, electronic **eavesdropping** sensors, and other means of detecting secret or hidden presence of humans and potentially dangerous substances. One advantage of equipment such as this is the broader use to which it can be put, including the detection of illegal drugs and substances.

In 2003 alone, drug smuggling networks were broken up, and almost 70 tons of cocaine were seized with 283 drug smugglers arrested by Homeland Security officers. The value of this haul on the streets of the United States would have been $4 billion. Frequently, drugs are involved in setting up funds to finance terrorist activity, and terrorist groups operating in the country might use this method to finance their work.

Fighting terror is as much about cleaning up the streets as it is about catching people blowing up buildings. Money obtained by the sale of drugs might be used to kill the very same people who sold the drugs in the first place. The elimination of illegal drug **trafficking** is vital to suppressing terrorist cells that, however unlikely, might choose to set up their money-making operations inside the United States.

Stopping the buildup of groups like these is an important part of defending the nation. **Aerial surveillance** has a role to play, but joint border operations are equally important. Various methods of detecting illegal immigrants crossing the border are set up to stem the flow of these aliens and to protect innocent lives.

A Department of Homeland Security UAV in flight over the Arizona-Mexico border.

Along with the US-VISIT program, border surveillance is a crucial step in plugging holes where unscrupulous and illegal immigrants get in to the country. To assist the lawful citizen making frequent trips back and forth across the Canadian and Mexican borders, security officers have established a system to speed the inspection process. Frequent crossers are screened for security purposes and are issued with passes that enable them to come and go on presentation of the card.

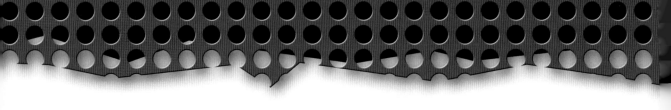

Chapter Five

Keeping the Freight Moving

When truckers move frequently between countries they need to cross borders with minimum delay. They too are screened

and, when cleared for frequent passes, their trucks are fitted with a special radio device that transmits information to Homeland Security stations. This enables the trucks to move through the border process in a matter of a few seconds rather then the hours it would take to check each driver and his or her freight load. It also eases traffic congestion and helps speed the flow at the busiest commercial land crossings.

The truckers use what are known as Free and Secure Trade (FAST) lanes, and new FAST radio check crossings are being added all the time. This reduces frustration and increases the efficiency of the screening process. Checking those people coming into the United States is frequently a time-consuming process, and the DHS has also increased the number of checking stations.

Moving goods and products manufactured abroad into the United States is an important part of trade with other countries

(Opposite) A customs officer demonstrates how FAST works to Secretary Ridge at the Bridge of the Americas in El Paso, Texas.

around the world. Across the globe, 80 percent of all goods moved in and out of countries travels on sea. The DHS wanted to speed up the process by which goods coming into the United

International cooperation is vital if we are to defeat international terrorism. Here U.S. and Chinese officials sign an agreement permitting pre-screening of containers from China destined for U.S. ports.

A U.S. Coast Guard patrol keeps a watchful eye on a container ship entering a U.S. port.

States could be checked for bombs, explosives, toxic substances, **biological** weapons and/or illegal immigrants.

By the end of its second year of operation, the DHS had set up a freight container screening process whereby 80 percent of all the goods coming into the United States were pre-screened before they left their country of origin. This significantly improves the ability to stop harmful substances, **weapons of mass destruction**, and poisonous substances from arriving at American ports.

The U.S. Coast Guard and the New York City police jointly patrol the New York Harbor area.

New maritime safety regulations give powers to the U.S. Coast Guard, which is responsible for patrolling the coasts and policing the new laws. These laws are widespread and extend to the ports overseas where goods leave to be transported to the United States. More than 100 foreign countries have been assessed for their port security, and strict guidelines are demanded of any country wanting to send goods to the United States.

Chapter Six

New Technology

More than 12,000 border patrol agents cover America's northern and southern land borders. To raise the level of technical effectiveness, UAVs and converted patrol aircraft are employed to maximize the efficiency and multiply the effectiveness of these patrol officials on the ground. In other areas new technology is not only a vital part of the war on terrorism, but it can also be used by the terrorists themselves. So there must be safeguards.

To develop new tools in the fight against terrorism, the DHS has invested heavily in research and technology by harnessing existing scientific and technical resources. These resources comprise existing government and institutional research facilities and are generated in new programs that link elements of the Department's science and technology directorate.

This directorate aims to develop state-of-the-art systems able to prevent, detect, and reduce the impact of mass attack by chemical, biological, **radioactive**, **nuclear**, and explosive attacks. It seeks to develop training procedures and to help support local law enforcement and emergency organizations in

In Newark, New Jersey, a customs inspector demonstrates how high-tech searching equipment can be used. The inset photo shows how X-ray scanning equipment can detect weapons carried inside a metal container.

times of crisis. It also helps build up the technical capabilities of the Department's link with other federal, state, local, and tribal agencies to dig down into their own concerns for protective measures and requirements for dealing with life-threatening events.

It is as much a part of the directorate's role to anticipate new and emerging threats as it is to develop new technology for the fight against terrorism. In every war, it is always wise to try to think like the enemy, to carry out research to see how a bomb or a toxic device could be made by terrorists. In that way the fight against terrorists anticipates new and clever ways in which weapons can be assembled and hidden, arming the security officers with information that informs them what to look for.

Enforcement officers need to wear special equipment when dealing with a chemical attack by terrorists.

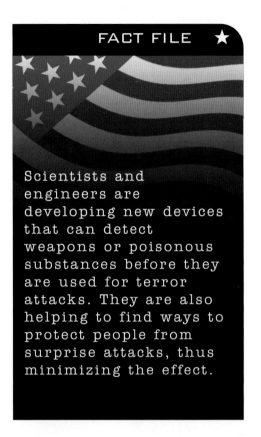

To mobilize the technical fight, the DHS has its own Homeland Security Advanced Research Projects Agency that works with private companies to develop new devices or produce new technology needed to fill gaps in the scientific or technical **arsenal**. Just a quick run through the agency's shopping list for new devices gives a feel for the sort of work they do: detection systems for nuclear countermeasures, **cyber security** research, instant **bio-aerosol detectors**, and many more.

The agency is even looking into the possibility of a really big attack using missiles and rockets fired at our homeland from locations outside the country. It is possible that some group or terrorist organization could mount a conventional missile on a ship and fire it from international waters directly at the United States. Such a missile could carry any one of the many different types of weapons of mass destruction and cause the deaths of millions of people. Defense against such attack is difficult but not impossible.

To achieve an early warning system for just such an attack, the DHS stops at nothing to construct an alert system involving surveillance from the air and from space. Satellites are used routinely by our government to spy and eavesdrop on terrorist organizations and on countries that provide safety for international criminals. Surveillance is also crucial to stopping ships that might be used by terrorists from reaching within range of the American coastline.

It is because homeland security needs the resources of the entire nation that the DHS effectively uses every known asset available to our government to find the threat and eliminate it. That sometimes means working closely with the Department of Defense or the Central Intelligence Agency, each of which has highly sophisticated devices for listening and looking.

This is a NATO Sea Sparrow missile being launched during a test in the Atlantic Ocean. The DHS is responsible for ensuring that weapons like these can never be fired at U.S. targets.

Chapter Seven

Advisory Systems

If the DHS believes there are threats from highly advanced weapons, it has links to these other departments and agencies to enlist their help. The response depends on the level of the threat, and the DHS functions in exactly that way.

The organization guides and coordinates preventive action by using all the resources at its disposal, and because there is no upper limit to that level it covers all contingencies. The DHS actively encourages a security advisory system and works with local leaders and with local government organizations to

The colors of the Homeland Security Advisory System.

A U.S. Coast Guard officer working with students at a school on Staten Island, New York. The DHS encourages cooperation among its various agencies and the public at all levels.

identify threats and to improve security. To accomplish this the DHS has set up an advisory rating updated daily to indicate varying levels of threat.

At the least risk is the *low* (green) category, indicating a low risk of terrorist attack. Next up comes the *guarded* (blue) rating, where there is a general risk of attack but nothing specific. Higher still is the *elevated* (yellow) level where there is believed to be a significant risk of some terrorist attack. Above that is the *high* (amber) alert level indicating a serious risk of attack. Highest of all is the *severe* (red) alert where an attack is believed to be imminent.

These advisory levels and their associated colors can be seen in federal and local government buildings and are used in general to communicate the state of risk for that day or in certain places. It serves as a cautionary notice that all citizens should observe, respect, and act accordingly. By color-coding the level of alert, people can be prepared. The impact of a surprise attack should thereby be minimized.

Advisory notices form an important part of collective responsibility, and the DHS works closely with organizations fighting crime, drug trafficking, and other activities set in motion by a minority. Schools are informed of threats to the personal security of students, and the police forces work closely with Department officials to coordinate preventive measures to safeguard children and young people.

The DHS has expanded its role since it formed and now includes a broader range of threats and a more inclusive group of local and national concerns relating to disasters. At a personal level, the DHS also provides appropriate people to counsel and support victims of terrorism and those who are relatives of people killed and injured by such events.

Chapter Eight

Resources and Funding

When the Department of Homeland Security was formed in March 2003 it had an annual budget of $31 billion, and that increased to $36.5 billion for fiscal year 2004 (beginning October 1, 2003). For fiscal year 2005, that budget ran at more than $40 billion and is likely to remain at that level for some time to come. It pays for all the coordinated activity of the DHS and for new directorates and sections of the Department to be added as necessary.

In 2005 the DHS set up a new domestic nuclear detection office; this is typical of the way in which the Department grows according to needs. The new office has a domestic detection and reporting system to alert officials to the illegal movement of nuclear devices into the United States, within the states, or illegally from one place to another.

Many other government departments are involved and include the Department of Energy, the Department of Defense, the Federal Bureau of Investigation, the Department of Justice, the Department of State, and the intelligence community. The movement of nuclear materials crucial to making weapons is a controlled activity, and electronic surveillance helps to keep track of these activities. The movement of dangerous substances in general is a concern to the security of the homeland.

The DHS has developed sophisticated electronic surveillance along the northern and southern land borders and has installed sensors and video surveillance to monitor illegal activity. This should go a long way to stop the movement of illegal aliens, terrorists, weapons of mass destruction, and contraband material—goods that enter without declaration, inspection,

At the port of Newark, New Jersey, a truck passes through a radiation portal. This machine is designed to detect radiological weapons.

An armed Coast Guard helicopter on patrol above Miami, Florida.

or import duty. New and innovative ways of catching the terrorists are being put into service all the time. Long-range **radar** is used by the Office of Air and Marine Operations to detect and intercept aircraft attempting to avoid detection while entering the United States.

Armed helicopters are based at Coast Guard stations and would be used to intercept surface ships or boats illegally landing on dispersed or remote areas of the coastline. Out at sea, an integrated deepwater system has been set up by the Coast Guard to improve security at sea-lane approaches and in ports.

Control of air defense forces is also an integral part of homeland security. All the detection and monitoring technology employed and coordinated by the DHS is backed up by the U.S. Air Force, which guards the air lanes of the U.S. civil air traffic system. We all use airlines to carry us safely and speedily around the country, and the safety of these transport systems is one of the most important features of diligent surveillance.

The U.S. Coast Guard is involved in an exercise to remove contraband or weapons of mass destruction from a container ship.

American civil air lanes are protected by planes from the U.S. Air Force. This F-15 Eagle is from the 445th Flight Test Squadron.

As the events of 9/11 have shown, it is easy for an aircraft to be turned into a destructive weapon. Only by having fighter patrols that can prevent events like those of 9/11 recurring can passengers travel safely and with confidence. The sky marshal program—where armed guards in plain clothes pose as passengers ready to overthrow terrorists—has been very successful, and passengers now expect a degree of policing in the air as well as on the ground.

Homeland security is about diligence and responsibility. Diligence is the service to the tasks and the duties that can help make our country a safer place. Responsibility comes with

Terrorists could strike anywhere people are gathered together. A Homeland Security marine unit patrols the 2005 Superbowl in Jacksonville, Florida.

Ensuring our freedom and safety a Bureau of Immigration and Customs helicopter patrols the skies over Washington, D.C.

freedom, and it is one of the most precious assets of our society. We all like to think that these are qualities that we as individuals bring to society. Homeland security is about nothing more than extending those qualities to our communities and to the greater benefit of our nation and its people.

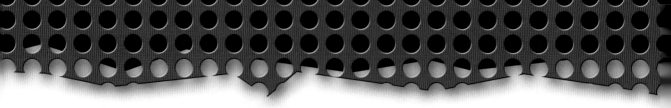

Glossary

aerial surveillance: watching an area from an airplane or satellite

arsenal: a collection of weapons or military equipment stored by a country, person, or group

bio-aerosol detectors: machines that can detect the presence of biological weapons

biological: relating to living things such as plants and animals

biometric: to do with the collection of statistical information about the biology of a living thing

counterfeit: a fake that has been made to like exactly like the real thing

cyber security: security of the Internet

eavesdropping: to secretly listen to someone else's conversation

fanatic: someone who is wildly enthusiastic about something such as a belief, a cause, or an interest

infiltrator: a person who secretly moves into another country or organization to spy and gain information

infrastructure: the base or foundation of an organization or system

nuclear: to do with the nucleus of an atom

radar: equipment that is used to detect things that are far away and to work out their position

radioactive: if an object is radioactive it gives off strong, often harmful, rays

reprisal: an act of revenge

trafficking: the illegal buying and selling of goods such as drugs and weapons

weapons of mass destruction: weapons capable of killing large numbers of people and creating huge amounts of damage

Further Reading

Binns, Tristan. *The CIA (Government Agencies)*. Sagebrush, 2002

Binns, Tristan. *The FBI (Government Agencies)*. Sagebrush, 2002

Brennan, Kristine. *The Chernobyl Nuclear Disaster (Great Disasters)*. Chelsea House, 2002

Campbell, Geoffrey A. *A Vulnerable America (Lucent Library of Homeland Security)*. Lucent, 2003

Donovan, Sandra. *How Government Works: Protecting America*. Lerner Publishing Group, 2004

Gow, Mary. *Attack on America: The Day the Twin Towers Collapsed (American Disasters)*. Enslow Publishers, 2002

Hasan, Tahara. *Anthrax Attacks Around the World (Terrorist Attacks)*. Rosen Publishing Group, 2003

Katz, Samuel M. *Global Counterstrike: International Counterterrorism (Terrorist Dossiers)*. Lerner Publishing Group, 2004

Katz, Samuel M. *Targeting Terror: Counterterrorist Raids (Terrorist Dossiers)*. Lerner Publishing Group, 2004

Katz, Samuel M. *U.S. Counterstrike: American Counterterrorism (Terrorist Dossiers)*. Lerner Publishing Group, 2004

Margulies, Phillip. *Al-Qaeda: Osama Bin Laden's Army of Terrorists (Inside the World's Most Infamous Terrorist Organizations)*. Rosen Publishing Group, 2003

Marquette, Scott. *America Under Attack (America at War)*. Rourke Publishing LLC, 2003

Morris, Neil. *The Atlas of Islam*. Barron's, 2003

Owen, David. *Hidden Secrets: A Complete History of Espionage and the Technology Used to Support It*. Firefly Books Ltd, 2002

Ritchie, Jason. *Iraq and the Fall of Saddam Hussein*. Oliver Press, 2003

Websites to visit

The Central Intelligence Agency:
www.cia.gov

The Department of Defense:
www.defenselink.mil

The Department of Homeland Security:
www.dhs.gov

The Federal Bureau of Investigation:
www.fbi.gov

The U.S. Air Force:
www.af.mil

The U.S. Army
www.army.mil

The U.S. Coast Guard:
www.uscg.mil

The U.S. Government Official Website:
www.firstgov.gov

The U.S. Marine Corps:
www.usmc.mil

The U.S. Navy:
www.navy.mil

The U.S. Secret Service:
www.secretservice.gov

The White House:
www.whitehouse.gov

Index